A Right Christmas Caper

A Play for Children

Willis Hall

SAMUEL FRENCH

FOUNDED 1830

SAMUELFRENCH-LONDON.CO.UK
SAMUELFRENCH.COM

A RIGHT CHRISTMAS CAPER

First performed at the Shaw Theatre, London, on 30th
November, 1977, with the following cast:

Convict Gilbert	Tom Owen
Convict Crosby	Mike Savage
Detective Constable Grummett	Stephen Lewis
Mr Mullins	David Weston
Mr MacBain	Johnny Wade
The Prison Governor	Bunny Reed
Clara Grummett	Jo Kendall
Alexander Grummett	Russell Gleed
The Ice-Cream Girl	Sue Bond

Directed by	Brian Rawlinson
Designed by	Dee Greenwood
Lighting by	Mark Jonathan

ACT ONE
Scene One—A Prison Yard
Scene Two—Detective Constable Grummett's Living-room

ACT TWO
Scene One—A Police Station
Scene Two—A Forest

ACT ONE

Scene One

*Two convicts, Gilbert and Crosby, are
trudging round and round the exercise yard
of a prison. In the centre of the yard stands
a stunted, leafless, little tree.*

*It is Christmas Eve and the prison yard is
bathed in moonlight. A notice proclaims: A
MERRY CHRISTMAS TO ALL OUR
CONVICTS. But it is a chill night and the
two prisoners are not feeling particularly
merry. Gilbert begins to sing in an attempt
to bolster his spirits.*

Gilbert (*singing*) While shepherds watched
     Their turnip tops
     A-boiling in the pot
     The Angel of the Lord flew down
     And scoffed the blinkin' lot . . .

Crosby Belt up, Gilbert.

    *The two convicts continue to plod round
    and round the tree. Gilbert manages to keep
    his silence for only a matter of seconds.*

Gilbert (*singing*) Oh Hell, O Hell,
     The Angels did shout
     When they fell down from Heaven
     And knocked themselves out . . .

Crosby I said, put a sock in it, Gilbert.
Gilbert I'm only trying to cheer us up, Crosby.
Crosby Don't bother.

    *They plod on. Two prison warders,
    Mullins and MacBain enter.*

Mullins Smartly does it, you felons. Keep moving! No
talking, and pick those feet up. Christmas Day
tomorrow remember. Right, Mr MacBain?
MacBain Christmas Day it is, Mr Mullins. And prison
Christmas Dinner for you two lucky lads at noon
tomorrow!

Crosby   What are we getting this year, Mr MacBain?
MacBain   The same as every year, Crosby. Stringy chicken,
           soggy sprouts, greasy gravy and cold mashed
           potatoes.
Crosby   Ugh!
Mullins   Lovely! Followed by sloppy Christmas pud and
           lumpy custard.
Gilbert   Agh!
MacBain   Delicious! Serves you right for being naughty. A
           Merry Christmas to you, Mr Mullins!
Mullins   Ditto, Mr MacBain—and a very happy New Year!
           I sincerely hope I have the pleasure of pulling a
           cracker or two with you before the night is out.
           Come on, you convicts, eyes front, chins in, chests
           out—let's see a spring in your step, lads. It is
           Christmas Eve, remember.
MacBain   It is indeed, Mr Mullins. And we ought to be on
           our way if we don't want to be late for the Prison
           Governor's sherry party.
Mullins   There'll be mince-pies, Mr MacBain!
MacBain   There'll be Christmas cake with icing and little
           plastic reindeers!
Gilbert   Are we getting any special treats tonight, Mr
           MacBain?
MacBain   If you behave yourselves—an extra digestive
           biscuit with your mug of cocoa.
Mullins   Stick at it, Gilbert and Crosby. Keep moving round
           the exercise yard. And let's see a happy smile on
           both your faces. It's the festive season!

                       *Mullins and MacBain go off singing 'God
                       rest you merry gentlemen'. Gilbert and
                       Crosby wait until the two warders are out
                       of sight and then they cease their
                       perambulations.*

Crosby   They've gone! Stringy chicken, soggy sprouts,
           greasy gravy, cold 'taties. I hate being in prison at
           Christmas, Gilbert. I do, I really hate it.
Gilbert   We could escape.
Crosby   From here? Tonight?
Gilbert   Why not? It's the best time of the year to escape.
           It's marvellous out in the world tonight, Crozz. It's

Christmas Eve. 'Ere, I'll bet if we did escape, we could find a *real* Christmas scene—instead of just this rotten prison scenery. There'll be shop windows, Crozzie, full of toys, all lit up, with the glass all steamy from kiddies' faces. And the streets out there will be full of cheerful people with enormous parcels. We might even find our very own tree.

Crosby   (*indicating the tree*) We've got a tree.

Gilbert   That's not a tree! A *real* tree, Crosby. With fairy lights and stars and shiny balls and tinsel and presents piled up underneath it. And it'd be *our* tree, Crozzie.

Crosby   I'm not sure about that, Gilbert.

Gilbert   How do you mean?

Crosby   It's not only Christmas Eve, Gilbert. (*He points above his head*) Look up there. It's full moon as well.

Gilbert   So what?

Crosby   So what? I'll tell you 'so what', Gilbert. I know where I like to be when it's full moon—Chrissy Eve or no Chrissy Eve—and that's safely locked up in my own little cell, warm and snug in my very own bed, with my head beneath the blankets.

Gilbert   What are you talking about?

Crosby   You know what comes out when it's full moon, Gilly?

Gilbert   (*shaking his head*) No.

Crosby   Yes, you do. I'll give you three guesses—go on, guess.

Gilbert   I haven't the faintest idea.

Crosby   Yes, you have. I hate it when you mess me about like this, Gillo. I do, I really hate it.

Gilbert   Is it Dracula?

Crosby   No. We had him last year— he doesn't need a full moon. He comes out of his coffin every night as soon as it's dark. Try again.

Gilbert   Frankenstein's monster?

Crosby   He was in the play the year before last. Doesn't time fly? No—it's somebody much worse than him.

Gilbert   I've no idea. Give me a clue.

Crosby   Somebody that's really horrible. And his face is all
          furry and so are his hands and feet.

Gilbert   It's not Paddington Bear, is it?

Crosby   No! (*Indicating the audience*) I'll bet they know.
          (*And then to the audience*) Who is it, kids, that
          only comes out when it's full moon and has an evil
          furry face and evil furry hands and feet? (*Audience:
          'Werewolf!' 'The Wolfman!'*) Who did you say?
          (*Audience: 'Werewolf', etc.*) That's him. There you
          are—the Werewolf.

Gilbert   A wolf where?

Crosby   A wolfman.

Gilbert   There's no such thing as a wolfman.

Crosby   Oh yes there is, Gillo, and every night when there's
          a full moon you can hear his evil unearthly
          bloodcurdling howling drifting on the still night air.

Gilbert   There isn't. There's no such person. He's just in
          stories. Somebody made him up.

Crosby   Are you sure, Gilly?

Gilbert   Absolutely certain. You don't want to be frightened
          by silly stupid things like that.

                    *At which point, we hear an unearthly
                    bloodcurdling howl drifting on the still
                    night air. Gilbert, terrified, leaps up into
                    Crosby's arms.*

          Ooo-er!

Crosby   Fantastic, Gilbert, you've done it again! Trust you
          to get it wrong. No such thing as a werewolf?
          What was that?

                    *Gilbert's courage begins to return. He gets
                    down from Crosby's arms.*

Gilbert   That wasn't the cry of the wolfman, Crozz.

Crosby   Wasn't it? It sounded like an evil unearthly
          bloodcurdling howl all right—and it was drifting on
          the still night air.

Gilbert   No, it was probably just the stage-manager,
          messing about with a sound effect. It was nothing
          to worry about.

Crosby   Oh no, nothing to worry about at all—I know this

much Gillo,—I'm staying where I am tonight. Wild horses wouldn't drag me out of this prison.

Gilbert You do what you like, Crosby. I'm going to make a break for it. I'm not stopping here one night longer. Wolfman or no Wolfman—if I have to listen to those warders and the Prison Governor sing 'Silent Night', one more time, just one more Christmas morning, I shall go raving mad. I'm off.

Crosby How are you going to get away?

Gilbert Dead simple. I shall create a diversion.

Crosby What a great idea, Gilbert! It's a fantastic idea, is that . . . (*He double-takes*) Create a what?

Gilbert A diversion. You know—I'll attract their attention somewhere else and while they're . . .

> *A raincoated figure approaches the stage from out of the audience. It is Detective Constable Grummett. He also wears large boots and a bowler hat.*

Grummett Oh, no, you won't, Gilbert!

Crosby Who are you?

Gilbert You're not allowed up here!

Grummett Yes, I am. I can go wherever I please. I have *carte blanche*. I am Detective Constable Grummett, C.I.D. I also happen to be a member of the audience.

Crosby It's him again!

Gilbert I don't know how he does it. He never misses a performance.

Grummett You're right, Gilbert. I don't. I come here regular to keep an eye on you two villains. (*He gets on to the stage*) I am also here as a *bona fide* representative of the Public Moral Code. I am here to see that what takes place upon this stage is right and proper family seasonal entertainment.

Gilbert There's nothing wrong with this play.

Grummett Pull the other one, Gilbert, it's got bells on it! Nothing wrong with the play? You mean there's nothing right with it! Bloodcurdling, unearthly, evil howls? Drifting on the still night air? Wolfmen? Convicts nipping over prison walls? Creating . . . what did you say you were going to create?

Gilbert   Only a diversion.

Grummett Disgraceful! I've got you this time, Gilbert and
         Crosby. I'm banning this entertainment.

Crosby   You can't do that, Detective Constable Grummett!

Grummett I've done it, Crosby. We're going to have something
         else instead.

Gilbert   Such as what?

Grummett Wait for it. This'll impress you. I'm going to
         personally organize something that is appropriate
         for the time of year, will entertain these kiddie-
         winkies, and something that can also be counted as
         educational and instructive.

Crosby   What is it, Detective Constable Grummett?

Grummett A Carol Concert.

Gilbert }
Crosby   } A what?

Grummett A Carol Concert.

Gilbert }
Crosby   } A Carol Concert?

Grummett You heard. Something a bit uplifting. (*To the
         audience*) You'd rather have a Carol Concert,
         wouldn't you? (*Audience: 'No!'*) Well, you're
         flippin' well getting one! You ignorant little horrors!
         Starting off with 'Silent Night', going into 'We
         Three Kings of Orient Are', and I haven't decided
         yet what comes after that one.

Gilbert   But we haven't got the right scenery for a Carol
         Concert, Detective Constable Grummett. This is
         prison scenery.

Grummett That's just where you're wrong, clever-clogs. This
         scenery ideally suits my purpose. 'Cos what we're
         going to have is a *Prison* Carol Concert. You
         convicts are going to sing some carols for the
         Governor and the warders. It'll make a smashin'
         evening's entertainment. Where is the Prison
         Governor?

Gilbert   Having a glass of Chrissy sherry with the warders.

Grummett Yes, of course he is! Do you happen to know if it's
         real sherry or theatrical sherry?

Crosby   How do you mean, Detective Constable Grummett?

Grummett What I say. Are they drinking real sherry out there, or prop sherry? I know what actors are—they stand up here pretending to be drinking real drink, and all the time it's just cold tea or something.

Gilbert   It's real sherry all right, Detective Constable Grummett. The Governor always has a bottle of proper sherry backstage every Christmas.

Grummett   Does he really? I'll nip along and join him then. While I'm gone, you two can make a start and get some rehearsing in on a couple of the golden oldies —'Good King Wenceslas' and 'Silent Night'. I'll probably get a couple of sherries when he hears about my Carol Concert.

Grummett goes off, breaking the little tree.

Crosby   A Carol Concert? A fizzin' Carol Concert! Look what he's done to our tree. I hate Detective Constable Grummett, Gilbert—I do, I really hate him! I hope it is cold tea!

Gilbert   Don't be like that, Crozz. He's given me a great idea.

Crosby   Not another of your ideas, Gilbert.

Gilbert   Why not?

Crosby   I don't think the world is ready for another of your ideas, Gillo.

Gilbert   You wait until you hear this one—you'll like it.

Crosby   Go on.

Gilbert   I'm going to use his Prison Carol Concert to create my diversion.

Crosby   Terrific, Gilly! How will you do that?

Gilbert   (*indicating the audience*) I'm going to get them to help me.

Crosby   The audience? All these kids? Help you to escape?

Gilbert   Yeah.

Crosby   How do you know they will?

Gilbert   I'll ask them. How about it, kids? Will you help me to get out of clink? (*Audience: 'Yes!'*) There you are!

Crosby   Great! Great! What do you want them to do, Gilly?

Gilbert   I'm going to get them all to join in the Carol Concert.

Crosby   Get all those kids to sing carols with us?
Gilbert   What's wrong with that?
Crosby   I hate Detective Constable Grummett, Gillo. And
           I'm not all that fond of the Prison Governor either.
           Why should we get all the kids to sing carols for
           them?
Gilbert   That's my *idea*, Crozzo. They're not going to sing
           proper carols—they're going to sing funny ones.
Crosby   What? With the wrong words?
Gilbert   Yes.
Crosby   Do you mean like: 'Good King Wenceslas knocked
           a bobby senseless, right in the middle of Marks and
           Spencers'—all like that?
Gilbert   (*nodding*) Yes.
Crosby   Fantastic! What a great idea, Gilly. The Prison
           Governor will go spare when he hears that at his
           Prison Carol Concert. He'll go stark raving bonkers.
           (*A sudden thought*) Hey! Hey! Hey! He'll blame
           Detective Constable Grummett for it!
Gilbert   I know.
Crosby   He'll think it was all Grummett's idea in the first
           place.
Gilbert   'Course he will. And then, while the governor is
           doing his nut, and spifflicating Detective Constable
           Grummett—that'll be my diversion. I shall make my
           escape.
Crosby   I'll come with you, Gilbert.
Gilbert   I thought you weren't going to escape from prison?
Crosby   I'm not going to let a great idea like yours go to
           waste. There's just one tiny thing though, Gilbert.
Gilbert   What's that?
Crosby   The audience doesn't know the words to your
           Chrissy carol.
Gilbert   They'll soon learn them. I've had them written
           down.
Crosby   What—on one of them big sheets that comes down
           from up there?
Gilbert   Yes. I know it's not entirely original, but it has been
           known to work.
Crosby   Not in the first scene, Gilly.
Gilbert   What do you mean?

Crosby   You never bring on the words of songs until the
          Second Act, Gilly. You never bring on the song-
          sheet in Christmas pantos until after the principal
          boy has won the hand of the beautiful principal
          girl. It's entirely against the laws of theatrical
          convention.

Gilbert   Oh, blow theatrical convention, Crosby. This is
          an emergency. (*Into the wings*) Can we have the
          song on please?

          *A sheet is dropped in from above, bearing
          the words of Gilbert's carol.*

Crosby   Oh, them's great words, Gilly! Terrific! I should
          think the Prison Governor will go blue in the face
          when he hears them.

Gilbert   I hope so, Crozz. Shall we have a rehearsal, kids?
          Are you ready? One—Two—Three . . .

All   While shepherds washed
          Their dirty socks
          And laid them out so neat
          The Angel of the Lord passed out
          When he smelled their sweaty feet!

Gilbert   What did you think, Crozz? . . . Crozz?

          *During the song, Crosby has had his eyes
          fixed on the song-sheet, his back to the
          audience. He is still singing it when the
          others finish.*

Crosby   Eh?
Gilbert   I said, what did you think of it?
Crosby   Have they sung it?
Gilbert   Just now.
Crosby   I didn't hear anything.
Gilbert   I think you'll have to try a bit harder, kids. Shall we
          have one more go? Really open your lungs this
          time. One—two—three . . .

All   While shepherds washed
          Their dirty socks
          And laid them out so neat
          The Angel of the Lord passed out
          When he smelled their sweaty feet!

Crosby   Great! Fantastic! I heard every word that time!

Gilbert   I should think the Prison Governor'll give Detective Constable Grummett what for when he hears you sing that.

The song-sheet disappears again.

Look out! I think they're coming. Look innocent, Crozz.

Gilbert and Crosby take up their positions for the carol concert, standing at attention and staring straight out at the audience. Detective Constable Grummett returns with the Prison Governor, who sports a large moustache.

Grummett   This way, Governor. I thought we'd hold the Prison Carol Concert out here in the exercise yard, sir.

Governor   What a jolly good idea, sergeant! It's an absolutely spiffing thought. A choir of convicts! Ha, ha, ha! Where are they, Grummett?

Grummett   These are they, Governor. Convicts Gilbert and Crosby.

Governor   (*a trifle disappointed*) Just the two of them?

Grummett   You know what it's like at Christmas, sir. It's difficult to lay your hands on spare convicts. Most of 'em are on absence of leave—acting in pantos up and down the country—taking the parts of wicked robbers or forty thieves or Abanazars and suchforth. These two'll do, sir. I'll get them to sing up and move about a bit so it'll look as if there's more of 'em.

Gilbert   Psst! Psst!

Grummett   Will you excuse me for a tiny moment, Governor? I think one of the altos wants a word with me.

Grummett crosses to Crosby. Gilbert is behind Crosby.

What is it?

Gilbert   While you were out, Detective Constable Grummett, we had a great idea.

Grummett   (*to Crosby*) You didn't move your lips. Oh yes? I'll believe that when I hear it.

Gilbert   It's about your Carol Concert. We can get the audience to sing with us.

Grummett (*glowering at the audience*) What? That ignorant
          lot of hooligans? Join in a Carol Concert? What
          makes you think they'll do it?
Gilbert   We've already asked them.
Grummett Really? And do you mean to tell me they've
          agreed? Stone me—wonders will never cease.
          There's hope for the world yet. (*He crosses back to
          the Governor*) Excuse me, Governor—permission to
          speak?
Governor Yes, Grummett?
Grummett I've just had rather a brilliant idea, sir.
Governor Go on?
Grummett Supposing we were to augment the choir with the
          voices of the audience?
Governor What a splendid wheeze, Grummett! Did you
          actually think of that yourself?
Grummett (*inclining his head, modestly*) I do 'ave 'em
          occasionally, Governor. They're not exactly
          convicts—yet—but the way they've been behaving,
          I hope to nick the lot of them before the
          entertainment's over (*To the audience*) I'll wipe
          those silly smiles off your faces with some solitary
          confinement and a Chrissy diet of bread and water!
          Now then, I'm going to conduct this Convicts'
          Carol Concert personally, so you'd better all sit up
          straight and behave yourselves. (*Back to the
          Governor*) Are you ready for your concert, sir?
Governor I can hardly wait, Grummett.
Grummett Then with your permission, sir . . .
Governor Proceed.

> *Grummett bows to the Governor formally, in
> the manner of a famous conductor, then
> crosses and takes up his position facing the
> audience. While he is doing this, and
> unnoticed by him, the song-sheet is
> dropped in again.*

Grummett (*out of the corner of his mouth*) What have I been
          practising, Crosby?
Crosby   'While Shepherds Watched', Detective Constable
          Grummett.
Grummett 'While Shepherds Watched'—when I count three.

(*To the Governor*) 'While Shepherds Watched', sir.
(*Back to the audience*) A-one—A-two—A-three!

Audience While shepherds washed
Their dirty socks
And laid them out so neat
The Angel of the Lord passed out
When he smelled their sweaty feet!

*During the singing of the above, Grummett
has become increasingly agitated at hearing
the wrong words. He runs up and down the
front of the stage, haranguing the audience.
The Governor also shows displeasure. In the
ensuing kerfuffle, Gilbert and Crosby effect
their escape into the auditorium.*

Grummett Shut up! Stop it! Stop messing about you little
horrors!

The song-sheet has disappeared again.

Governor Was that your idea of a joke, Grummett?

Grummett No, sir—it wasn't, sir—not me, sir. But I've a very
good idea who it *was*—it was these two
villainous . . . (*At which point he realizes that
Gilbert and Crosby are no longer present*) Good
Lor! They've gone, sir!

Governor Gone?

Grummett Gone—gone!, They've vamoosed . . .! (*He spots
them in the auditorium*)

*Grummett produces his whistle and blows
several short, sharp blasts on it. Mullins and
MacBain enter at the double.*

Grummett After them, lads! Smartly does it—get after those
two desperate criminals! Chop-chop—at the
double!

*Mullins and MacBain leap off the stage and
pursue Gilbert and Crosby through the stalls.
The two convicts make good their escape and
disappear into the foyer, pursued by the two
warders. Grummett regains the attention of
the audience.*

Grummett All right! Face front! Look at me, you horrible little monsters! I saw you! I spotted you assisting them two convicts *and* interfering with my two assistants while they were acting in the course of their duty! Permission to arrest the entire audience, Governor?

Governor Don't be an idiot, Grummett! Never mind the audience. Two convicts have got away.

Grummett Indeed they have, Governor. But fear not, sir. My lads will have the villains back in no time. Don't you worry.

Governor I don't intend to, Grummett. You're the one that's going to do the worrying. This was a happy little play about Christmas Day in a prison, until you stuck your big long nose in where it wasn't wanted. Carol Concert indeed! If those two prisoners aren't recaptured, Grummett, and double-quick, I shall ring Scotland Yard and speak to your superior officer.

Grummett You wouldn't do that, sir.

Governor I would. I will. I'll have you back in uniform and playing Ernest the Policeman in a provincial tour of 'Tales of Toytown'.

The Governor stalks off. Grummett follows him.

Grummett No, sir. Not that, sir. Anything but that, sir!

Mullins and MacBain enter, out of breath.

MacBain Lost 'em, Mr Mullins.

Mullins We always do, Mr MacBain. Every year, we lose 'em in the audience.

MacBain It's beginning to get me down, Mr Mullins.

Mullins Don't say that, Mr MacBain. It's a grand life, acting the part of an officer in Her Majesty's Prison Service. It's better than playing police constables.

MacBain We were constables in last year's panto.

Mullins We were all sorts last year. We were constables, we were guardsmen—we even played a panto horse!

MacBain I enjoyed that!

They assume their panto-horse positions and gallop around the stage

I wouldn't say 'no' to playing a panto horse again, if ever the opportunity arose.

Mullins   I'll tell you what I *didn't* like about last year's panto.

MacBain   Go on?

Mullins   The grinning green skelligog. That really put the wind up me.

MacBain   I don't remember that one.

Mullins   Yes, you do. You must do. When all the audience went 'Whee!' and this grinning green skelligog came on. It gave me the shivering ab-dabs.

MacBain   (*shaking his head*) No, I don't remember that at all. Will you refresh my memory?

Mullins   Is that wise?

MacBain   (*addressing the audience*) Would you like to do it now, kids? When I say 'Go' you all say 'Whee!' and see if it stirs my memory. Ready? Go!

> *Unnoticed by MacBain, a grinning green skeleton descends and jiggles in front of Mullins. Mullins is struck speechless and suffers an attack of the shivering ab-dabs. As the skeleton disappears again, MacBain turns back to Mullins. He fails to notice his comrade's distressed condition.*

MacBain   Are you all right, Mr Mullins? I've just remembered. It wasn't 'Whee!'. it was 'Whoo!'. And it wasn't a grinning green skelligog either—it was a horrible hairy spider.

Mullins   I've no recollection of that at all.

MacBain   (*moving downstage*) Shall we try it, kids? When I say 'Go!' all shout 'Whoo!' Go!

> *Unnoticed by MacBain, a horrible, hairy spider descends and dangles in front of Mullins, striking him dumb with fear and giving him the screaming jim-jams. After the spider disappears, Gilbert and Crosby are seen trying to sneak furtively across the stage.*

Mullins   The missing convicts, Mr MacBain! After 'em!

> *The two warders, blowing short, sharp blasts on their whistles, pursue the convicts again, through the audience and out into the auditorium. Dectective Constable Grummett*

enters and blows his whistle to gain the audience's attention.

Grummett I was watching that, you rotten little monsters. Don't think, I didn't see you, going 'Whee!' and 'Whoo!' and fetching on skelligogs and spiders. And you big ones are just as bad. And if none of you grown-ups can't control the kids—I shall take certain steps to do the job myself. I've got friends in high places. I shall speak to a chum of mine who's a chum of a chum of the man who blots the copy-book of the Minister of Education. He'll settle your lot's hash all right. He'll get a couple of days knocked off your Chrissy holidays! I'll have your school dinners cancelled! (*A fiendish laugh*) That'll teach you! That'll serve you right. You won't get the better of Detective Constable Grummett very easily.

Grummett turns to leave but, before he can do so, Clara Grummett, his wife, approaches the stage from the back of the auditorium. She is trundling a shopping trolley.

Clara Stephen! Stephen Grummett!

Grummett Clara! My own darling Clara! (*To the audience*) This is as much a surprise to me as it is to you. Allow me to introduce the wife—Clara, my love, this is the audience.

Clara Grummett casts a peremptory glance over the audience.

Clara Merry Christmas. How do you do? (*Then back to Grummett*) I can't let you out of my sight for an instant, can I, Stephen?

Grummett (*to the audience*) Excuse me one moment. (*Back to Clara*) What do you mean, dearest? What are you doing here, in the theatre?

Clara The very question, Stephen, that I was about to ask you.

Grummett I'm here on official business, Clara.

Clara You're supposed to be off duty.

Grummett A policeman is never off duty, Clara.

Clara You gave me to understand that you were going into town to make some last-minute seasonal purchases. You told me, quite specifically, that you were going out to get a sprig of mistletoe, a half-pound bag of Brazil nuts, and some stocking-fillers for little Alexander.

Grummett And so I am, beloved. Post-haste.

Clara Then what are you doing here? I popped down to the butcher's to collect the turkey for tomorrow. (*She holds up her shopping trolley*) I have it here. And something *told* me to look inside this theatre. Why did you come into the building, Stephen? What makes you do it? It happens every year.

Grummett Only my copper's sense of duty, Clara. I like to make sure that the panto's up to scratch, that's all, and not a load of old rubbish, and it is rubbish. It's a good job I did come in—I'm trying to turn it into a Carol Concert. 'Christians Awake', and 'Away In A Manger'. (*To the audience*) That's what you want isn't it, kids?

Audience No!

Grummett Shurrup, you ignorant hooligans! I'll decide what's best for you!

> *Clara makes a move to clamber up on the stage.*

Clara, you're trespassing on the stage! It's out of bounds to members of the audience. The only people allowed up here are actors, criminals playing the parts of actors, and plain-clothes detectives representing the Arts Council. You can't come up here, my dear.

Clara We'll see about that.

> *Clara is on the stage.*

Grummett But you're supposed to be at home, Clara. Attending to that myriad of last-minute festive details—wrapping up prezzies; hoovering the living-room carpet; picking up the Chrissy cards that have fallen down into the fireplace from off the mantelpiece. You should be home, dear.

> *Clara points a dramatic finger at the set which has appeared behind them and now lights up.*

Clara That *is* my home, Stephen.

> *Grummett and Clara move into the set.*

Scene Two

The Grummett family's living-room. A small, neat room which is festooned with Christmas decorations. There is a window in the rear wall and a door which opens on to the hall. There is a fireplace with Christmas cards on the mantelpiece. There is a Christmas tree with presents underneath. A pillow-case hangs above the fireplace. Grummett and Clara enter the room.

Grummett You're right, Clara.

Clara What's going on? Is this your idea of a joke?

Grummett I'm as baffled as you are, dear. But I most definitely recognize those plaster ducks. And this armchair is decidedly familiar.

Clara goes out into the hall and returns without the shopping trolley.

Clara And that's our hall out there—it's got our wallpaper. Aw, and look, Stephen, there's dear little Alexander's pillow-case—bless him—hanging up for Santa Claus to pop his prezzies in!

Grummett And there's the very fleecy-lined mittens and slippers you're surprising me with tomorrow morning! (*He takes down a Christmas card from the mantelpiece*) And if further proof be needed— here it is. The Christmas card my superintendent sent us. 'A Merry Xmas, Detective Constable and Missis Grummett' written on the inside, and a perky robin sitting on a pair of handcuffs on the front. Is there no end to theatrical ingenuity? You know what all this means, Clara?

Clara What?

Grummett There may be room for criticism of the content of this play—but the stage-management is faultless! This is a perfect replica of our living-room!

Clara This *is* our living-room, Stephen.

Grummett God bless my soul! But what's it doing here?

Clara It must be part of the plot.

Grummett Never! Not my home. Not while there is breath in

my body, Clara. We couldn't hold a Convicts' Carol Concert in our living-room it isn't big enough. Besides, you wouldn't stand for the hobnail bootmarks on the hall lino.

Clara There's more to the plot of this play than a Convicts' Carol Concert, Stephen.

Grummett Not if Detective Constable Grummett has a hand in it. And I'm certainly not having you mixed up in a load of codswallop about Gilbert and Crosby.

Clara Gilbert and Crosby? Who are they?

Grummett A couple of desperate criminals I've had to cross swords with on previous occasions.

Clara Desperate criminals? *Real* desperate criminals?

Grummett That's what I keep trying to tell you. They've escaped from prison. Not only that, but they took the mickey out of my Carol Concert. (*Indicating the audience*) Aided and abetted, I might add, by that lot of badly brought up hooligans. (*Addressing the audience*) But don't think you're going to get away with it—before this panto's finished, I'll have the lot of you eating your dinner in remand homes! (*Back to Clara*) You see the type of person I have to deal with? But you're not getting mixed up with this one, Clara. You're going home.

Clara But I am home, Stephen. My place is at your side. In this perfect replica of our living-room.

Grummett Wait one tiny moment! What about our little lad, Alexander? We can't leave him alone on Christmas Eve while we go gallivanting in a seasonal entertainment.

Clara How do we know that he isn't here?

Grummett What? Our Alexander? Here? (*Indicating the audience*) In this theatre? Clara, you don't suppose that, even as we speak, he might be sitting out there in amongst those common little ruffians, watching a play that isn't fit for common little ruffians?

Clara I sincerely hope not—but, well, he may be, Stephen.

Grummett If you're out there, lad—sit tight, keep shtum, say nothing—I'll have you out of the clutches of those hooligans before you can say Dick Whittington.

*At which point, Alexander bursts into the
living-room through the hall door.*

Alexander I'm here, Dad! I've got a part in it!

Clara   Mummy's little angel!

Grummett Alexander, is it really you—or is it a perfect replica
            of his father's lad?

Alexander It's really me, Dad. I can prove it. Look—I'll pinch
            you.

He does so.

Grummett Ow!

Alexander Can I be in it, Dad? Can I? Can I be in it?

Grummett No, certainly not.

Alexander Go on, Dad. Let me.

Clara   Alexy-Walexy must do as Daddy-Waddy tells him.
            Goodness gracious, Mummy's little pet, this is no
            kind of play for a nicely brought up little boy to be
            in. It's about a prison breakout, lovey, *and* there's a
            werewolf in it.

Alexander Is there? Is there? Is there really, Dad? Is there a
            fiendish wolfman with dripping fangs and
            bloodshot eyes and is his hands and feet and face
            all hairy and horrible? Can I get him for you, Dad?

Grummett No!

Alexander I'll bet he's just an actor with a mask on. I'll kick
            his shins, I'll stamp on his toes, I'll bash him in the
            gut, I'll gouge his eyes out for you. Can I, Dad?
            Please! Can I gouge his eyes out?

Grummett How many more times, sonny—*No!*

Clara   Daddy knows best, Alex. Mummy's precious baby
            should be tucked up safe and snug in his little bed,
            cuddling his bendy Hitler doll and dreaming dreams
            about bullying smaller golden-headed children—
            you're much too young to be in a Christmas panto.

Alexander Aw . . . go on, Dad, let me.

Grummett Your mother's right. If the GLC got wind of the
            fact that you were acting under age, there'd be hell
            to pay.

Alexander *Please*, Dad . . .

Grummett Have I got to put my foot down fairly and squarely?
            Listen—if you aren't through that door, up them
            stairs, and into kip in that perfect replica of your

                    bedroom in ten seconds flat—there'll be no
                    Christmas prezzies in your pillow-case tomorrow
                    morning.
Alexander Aw, *Mum* . . .
Clara   Beddy-byes time, Mummy's poppett.
Alexander Oh—all right. But only if you promise me that Santa
                    Claus is bringing me a Martian deathray pistol,
                    and a razor-sharp Samurai sword, *and* a South
                    American headhunter's blowpipe with some
                    poisoned arrows. *And* a skateboard!
Clara   Mummy's darling must wait and see what Father
                    Christmas has in his sack for him. I'm sure he won't
                    forget the deathray pistol *or* the Samurai sword, *or*
                    the blowpipe with the poisoned arrows. But
                    Mummy's darlingest angel isn't getting a skateboard
                    this year—skateboards are dangerous.
Alexander *Aw* . . . Go on, Mum.
Grummett   You heard, son—scoot! Off to bed before I clip you
                    round the earhole. Merry Christmas, son—buzz off.

Alexander goes out.

Clara   Bless his little cotton socks.
Grummett   He's not a bad lad, is he, Clara? Although I says it as
                    shouldn't. I'd like to give him an extra special treat
                    this Christmas. Here—I'll tell you what!
Clara   Yes, Stephen?
Grummett   If I can recapture them missing convicts, get
                    somebody to organize some proper panto scenery
                    —(*he indicates the audience*)—our Alexander
                    could pop downstairs for my Convicts' Carol
                    Concert.
Clara   He'd enjoy that, Stephen!

Grummett addresses the audience.

Grummett   Wouldn't you like that too? Wouldn't you lot like to
                    stand up straight like good little boys and girls and
                    sing the 'Holly And The Ivy' for my little Alexander?
Audience   *No!*
Grummett   You rotten disgraceful little monsters!
Clara   What a badly brought up audience!
Grummett   If you want my honest opinion, Clara—I don't
                    think they are a *bona fide* theatrical audience.

Clara   Really? What are they, Stephen?

Grummett   I think they're a couple of bus-loads of football
            hooligans that have come here because they're
            banned at Chelsea.

            *At which point, we hear Alexander calling
            from his bedroom.*

Alexander   (*off*) Mum! *Mum!*

Clara   (*to Grummett*) Sshh! (*She tiptoes across and opens
            the door*) Wasn't that our Alexander?

Grummett   He wants a drink of water.

Alexander   (*off*) Mum! *Mum!* I want a drink of water!

Clara   (*to the audience*) Aw! Mummy's little angel's
            thirsty. Bless him! Isn't he a little treasure?
            Altogether, kiddies, shout with me—'Mumsie's
            coming Alexy-Walexy!' Mumsie's coming,
            Alexy-Walexey!

            *Various catcalls from the audience as Clara
            goes out again.*

Grummett   (*to the audience*) Which one of you little devils
            blew a raspberry? Somebody did—I distinctly
            heard it. I've half a mind to call this whole
            performance off. It's no skin off my nose. I'm
            seriously considering taking the entire cast of this
            play across the road to St Pancras Station. I could
            organize my Carol Concert on the station forecourt.
            The ten-forty-two from Luton is due in at any
            minute. The passengers off that would make a
            better audience than you disreputable wretches!

            Clara returns and peers round the hall door.

Clara   Stephen!

Grummett   Yes, my dear?

Clara   Do come and look! The theatre management have
            spared no expense this Christmas. There's our
            Alexander sitting up in a perfect replica of his little
            bed, as snug as a bug in a rug in a perfect replica
            of all his bedclothes! It's ever so sweet! Can you
            spare a minute?

Grummett   Yes, dear!

            Grummett and Clara go out into the hall.

*Gilbert and Crosby approach the stage from
the rear of the auditorium.*

Gilbert   Come on, Crozz. Mind the steps. I'll lead the way.

Crosby   Do you think we've given them the slip?

Gilbert   Who? Them two warders?

Crosby   Yes. Mr Mullins and Mr MacBain. Have we
managed to shake them off our tails?

Gilbert   Don't worry. We won't set eyes on them for a
scene or two, Crozzo. The last time I saw Mr
MacBain he was having a bitter quarrel with the
theatre barman in the foyer.

Crosby   What about?

Gilbert   He'd ordered a bottle of Guinness and he was
trying to pay for it with stage money.

Crosby   Great! He'll duff him up, that barman. What about
Mr Mullins?

Gilbert   He won't bother us either. He was having an
argument with the usherette—she won't let him
back into the auditorium unless he buys a ticket.

Crosby   Not the usherette at the top of the stairs?

Gilbert   (*nodding*) Do you know her?

Crosby   (*also nodding*) She doesn't stand for any nonsense.
She'll belt him with her torch if he gets awkward.
I should think we can get on with the play, Gilly,
and not worry about them warders.

*They pause as, for the first time, they see
the living-room set on the stage.*

Hey, Gillo! Look!

Gilbert   Aw! Isn't it smashing, Crozz? The feller who made
that scenery knew what he was doing! You can
easy tell it's a Chrissy play, can't you? Look at that
tree—*and* them decorations! 'Ere, Crozzie—I 'ent
half going to enjoy acting in this scenery.

*Gilbert and Crosby enter the living-room
set. Gilbert makes himself comfortable in
the armchair. Crosby gazes round the room.*

Gilbert   'Ere, this is it, eh, Crozzie? An actor's life for me,
old lad.

*Crosby is eyeing the living-room rather
doubtfully.*

Crosby	I *suppose* it's all right, Gilbert?
Gilbert	You *suppose*? This is what I *call* acting, Crozz. Sitting-down acting. A comfy armchair, a nice warm cosy fire. Hey—and Crozz, look under the tree!
Crosby	What at?
Gilbert	There's a pair of brand-new fleecy-lined Marks and Sparks, slippers. (*He puts on the slippers*)
Crosby	You're not going to put them on your feet?
Gilbert	'Course I am—I'd look silly with them on my head.
Crosby	I'll bet they're somebody's Chrissy present.
Gilbert	They are, Crozz—mine. First come, first served. Why don't you find something?
Crosby	I'm not touching anything in this house that doesn't belong to me, Gilbert.
Gilbert	I thought you were supposed to be a desperate criminal.
Crosby	So I am. I'm very desperate indeed. I should think I'm much more desperate than you are.

Crosby stoops and examines the presents.

Gilbert	Look, a pair of fleecy-lined mittens, Crozzie.
Crosby	Do you think I should?
Gilbert	Go on, surprise yourself. Be a devil—just for once. It's only for lends—it isn't really nicking—we can put them back before we go.

Crosby hesitates, but temptation wins.

Crosby	All right—I will.

Crosby slips on the sheepskin mittens.

They're great, these mittens, Gilly. They're just my size.

Gilbert	These slippers are terrific, Crozz—they could've been made for me.
Crosby	So's these.

They admire their new possessions. Gilbert stretches out his legs and wiggles his toes. Crosby extends his arms and wiggles his fingers.

Smashing!

Crosby's attention is drawn to something on the mantelpiece. Gilbert's eyes have strayed to a book on the sidetable. Crosby picks up the Christmas card. Gilbert studies the book.

Crosby   I say—Gilly? . . . Gillo!
Gilbert   (*preoccupied*) Mmmmm?
Crosby   Whose living-room is this, do you think?
Gilbert   Dunno.
Crosby   Would you give me an honest answer to an honest question?
Gilbert   If I can.
Crosby   What sort of a feller, in your opinion, would get a Christmas card with a picture of a robin sitting on a pair of handcuffs covered in snow?
Gilbert   I've no idea. Who do you reckon would read *The Bumper Christmas Annual of Unsolved Crimes*?
Crosby   I haven't a clue.

They exchange a long, thoughtful glance.

Gilbert   Are you thinking what I'm thinking, Crosby?
Crosby   I sincerely hope not, Gillo.
Gilbert   There's one certain way of finding out.
Crosby   Go on?
          Gilbert fishes a folded programme from his pocket.

Gilbert   It will tell us where we are in here.
Crosby   Why? How? What is it, Gilbert?
Gilbert   It's a programme, Crozz. I got it from a programme lady when I was in the foyer.
Crosby   A programme? Do you mean like Tottenham Hotspurs versus Wolves or QPR versus Liverpool?

Gilbert has unfolded his programme.

Gilbert   No, you silly nana. A theatre programme. For this theatre. For this play. It tells you everybody who is in it and where we are.
Crosby   Has it got me in there?
Gilbert   We're *all* in here. (*He consults the programme*) Look—this is you. Crosby, a convict, played by—— (*He reads the actor's name*)

Crosby   Who?

> *Gilbert reads the name again.*

Never heard of him. Who have they got to take the part of you? (*He snatches the programme from Gilbert and studies it*) I've never heard of him either. I've never heard of any of them on here. Is this the best they could afford?

> *Gilbert snatches the programme back again.*

Gilbert   Never mind the actors, Crosby. It's where we are that's more important now. (*He again consults the programme*) Scene One: A Prison Yard . . .

Crosby   I remember that scene, Gilbert. We escaped from there.

Gilbert   Scene Two—— Oh, cripes!

Crosby   What's up?

Gilbert   You're not going to like this when I tell you.

Crosby   Go on.

Gilbert   Scene Two: Detective Constable Grummett's Living-room.

Crosby   You're kidding me, aren't you, Gilly?

> *Gilbert shakes his head.*

Yes, you are. Tell the truth. You're pulling my leg— you're having me on.

Gilbert   (*shaking his head*) Look for yourself.

> *Crosby looks at the programme and then his eyes gaze wildly round the room as though seeking corroboration. He bolts for the door.*

Crosby   Come on!

Gilbert   Where to?

Crosby   Out of this scenery—where do you think?—as fast as our legs can carry us!

Gilbert   Where to?

Crosby   I don't *care* where to, Gillo. As long as we get out of here and give the stagehands a chance to get rid of this scenery. Detective Constable Grummett's living-room? We'd be better off on an empty stage! Are you ready?

　　　　　　　　　　A RIGHT CHRISTMAS CAPER

Crosby opens the hall door. As he does so, we hear again the unearthly bloodcurdling howl of the Werewolf. Crosby closes the door again, smartly.

Crosby　That's put the kybosh on it! We can't go out there neither.

Gilbert　Oooh heck!

Crosby　You silly, stupid twit, Gilbert!

Gilbert　What have I done?

Crosby　Don't pretend, Gillo—you *know* what you've done. What did I say to you in Scene One: A Prison Yard? I *said* we were better off in the nick, didn't I?

Gilbert　I don't remember.

Crosby　Oh yes, you do. But, oh no, you wouldn't have it. Look at the diabolical plot you've got us into now! Stuck in here in Detective Constable Grummett's house. And we can't go out because there's an evil, furry-faced wolfman, with dripping fangs, prowling about the stage.

Gilbert　Calm down, Crozz. There's no need to make a fuss.

Crosby　What! No need to make a fuss, isn't there? I suppose everything in the garden's lovely?

Gilbert　Keep your wool on, Crosby.

Crosby　You heard that evil, unearthly howl, didn't you— drifting on the still night air?

Gilbert　There isn't a werewolf out there, Crosby. It's just a sound effect.

Crosby　But it didn't sound like a sound effect to me. It sounded like a one hundred per cent genuine twenty-four carat werewolf's howl, did that.

Gilbert　Do you want me to prove it was sound effect?

Crosby　I'd be eternally grateful if you could.

Gilbert　You're not frightened of werewolves, are you, Crozz?

Crosby　No, no. I'm flippin' petrified!

Gilbert　Take another look at that programme then.

Crosby　What good will that do?

Gilbert　It'll prove to you that there isn't a werewolf in this panto.

Crosby　How?

Gilbert   You are thick, Crosby, when you want to be. If
            there really *is* a werewolf, his name will be in the
            programme, won't it?
Crosby   Will it?
Gilbert   Of course it will. It would have to be—by law—*and*
            the name of the actor who was portraying it. Go on
            then, you look down the programme, and tell me if
            you can find a werewolf on it.
Crosby   You're absolutely right, Gilly. There's no Mr
            Werewolf written down here.
Gilbert   And what does that mean, Crosby?
Crosby   There isn't a werewolf in the panto . . .

> *Again we hear the howl of the Werewolf and
> Crosby is suddenly not so sure.*

            . . . is there?
Gilbert   If it's name's not on the programme it's not in the
            panto, Crosby. Definitely.
Crosby   Hang about. Supposing it wasn't an actor playing a
            werewolf? Supposing it was a real werewolf?
Gilbert   It'd still be in the programme, Crozz. It would say:
            Werewolf, played by itself.
Crosby   I do believe you, Gilbert. You've convinced me.

> *The Werewolf's howl is heard again, louder
> than before. Crosby doesn't move a muscle.*

            I'm not frightened of that, Gillo. Sound effects
            don't scare me.
Gilbert   That's the spirit, Crosby. Everybody *knows*
            there aren't any monsters in pantos anyway. If
            there was, do you know what we'd probably see?
Crosby   Will it frighten me if you tell me?
Gilbert   No. Because it isn't going to happen, is it? If there
            really *was* a werewolf in this panto, Crozzie—he'd
            come creeping in at the dead of night and press his
            face up against the window!
Crosby   He would, he would, wouldn't he? And it would be
            all evil and furry!
Gilbert   Yeh, yeh! With these bloodshot eyes and dripping
            fangs!
Crosby   Ooooh, wouldn't it be scary!
Gilbert   Yeh! *And* creepy!

*At which point, and unnoticed by Gilbert
and Crosby, a werewolf's face appears at
the window. The audience go wild. The
Werewolf disappears.*

Crosby   (*after order has been restored*) There was a what,
            kids?
Audience   A werewolf!
Gilbert   A werewolf?
Audience   Yes!
Gilbert   No, there wasn't!
Audience   Yes, there was!
Gilbert   No, there wasn't. Don't believe them, Crozz. They're
            having you on. (*To the audience*) You're trying to
            put the wind up poor old Crosby, aren't you?
Audience   No!
Gilbert   Yes, you are. You know very well he doesn't like
            wolfmen, so you're doing it on purpose.
Crosby   You're right, Gillo. There isn't really a wolfman, is
            there?
Audience   There is! There is! Etc.
Gilbert   All right then, the next time you see a werewolf you
            tell us where he is.

            *At which point, the Werewolf returns and
            peers in at the window. The cries of the
            audience direct the convicts' attention to
            the grimacing figure outside. Gilbert and
            Crosby are suitably alarmed. The Werewolf
            disappears again.*

            I believe you now, kids! Hey, he's really evil, isn't
            he?
Crosby   Oh, Gilly. What are we going to do if he comes in
            through that door?
Gilbert   It won't come in here, Crozz. Don't worry.
Crosby   It will! It will! I've seen scenes like this in old
            horror films. First of all, you'll see that door-handle
            start to move, as the wolfman rattles it from outside.
Gilbert   It won't do that—will it?
Crosby   It will! It will! Then the door will creak open,
            slowly, and that monster will leap into the room
            and spifflicate the both of us!

Gilbert   It won't, Crozz. If it does—we'll catch it.
Crosby   What? Catch a werewolf? You've got to be joking,
            Gilbert!
Gilbert   (*picking up Alexander's pillow-case from the
            mantelpiece*) With this.
Crosby   What do you think you're going to do with that—
            lash him to death?
Gilbert   Listen, Crozz—as soon as that door starts to open,
            you switch out the light. And I'll stand on this chair,
            over here—(*he moves a chair near the door*)—and
            when the werewolf comes in, I'll pull the pillow-case
            down over its head.
Crosby   Hey, that's not bad, Gilly. I like that!
Gilbert   (*picking up a hefty ornament and handing it to
            Crosby*) Then, as soon as I've got the pillow-case
            over him, you bop him on the nut with this.
Crosby   Do you want to know something, Gilbert—I don't
            usually go along with your ideas, but I think you've
            managed to pull a good one out at last.

            *The door-handle has started to move. the
            audience will no doubt draw the convicts'
            attention to this fact.*

Crosby   Look, Gilbert—look!
Gilbert   (*to the audience*) Shh! Quiet, kids! Everybody,
            quiet—not a sound. Come on, Crozz. Don't forget.
            As soon as he opens the door, lights out first, then
            I get him with the pillow-case, then you bop him on
            the nut.
Crosby   As soon as you say the word, Gilly.

            *Gilbert climbs up on his chair. Crosby
            positions himself by the light switch and
            takes a firm grip on his ornament. The
            door-handle moves again. The door opens—
            slowly.*

Gilbert   Light, Crozz!

            *Crosby switches out the light. There is the
            sound of a scuffle in the darkness, and we
            hear a voice cry out.*

Voice   Ouch! *Ow!*

Gilbert   We've got him, Crozz! Give him another one for
             luck!
Voice   Oooh!
                      *The light is switched on. A figure is
                      staggering around the room, its head and
                      shoulders encased in a pillow-case,
                      moaning and clutching its head. The figure
                      is recognizable by its boots. It is Detective
                      Constable Grummett.*

Gilbert ⎫
Crosby   ⎬ Detective Constable Grummett!

Gilbert   Run for it, Crozz! Hide! Hide!
Crosby   Hide where, Gilbert? There isn't time!
Gilbert   There is, Crozz. We're in luck—the Interval's coming
             up.
                      *Gilbert and Crosby flee as Grummett
                      manages to free himself from the pillow-case.
                      There is a large dent in his bowler hat. He
                      addresses the audience.*

Grummett You horrible hairy little monsters! (*He takes off his
             bowler hat and feels the top of his head, gingerly*)
             Just wait till after the Interval. I'll get my own
             back—there'll be no more panto—I'll have you
             spelling and doing sums!

                      *Grummett jams his dented bowler firmly on
                      his head and turns to leave. The Werewolf
                      appears at the door and Grummett very
                      nearly jumps out of his skin.*

             Yee-OW! Mother!

                      Grummett races off the stage.

END OF ACT ONE

ACT TWO

Scene One

The stage is set as we left it at the end of Act One: the Grummett living-room.

As the house lights fade down, Detective Constable Grummett enters from the wings, stands in front of the living-room set, and addresses the audience.

Grummett There's a one-eyed yellow idol, to the north of Katmandu
There's a little marble cross beneath the town.
Right then—stop fidgeting, sit up straight and pay attention! Before the second half of this entertainment can continue, I have to make a very sad and serious announcement. This is it, so let's have total hush. It's about the Carol Concert. We've had to cancel it. Altogether—everybody say 'Aw!'

Audience Aw—etc.

Grummett Who said 'Hooray!'? Which one of you horrible little ragamuffins cheered? I'll have the whole caboodle of you doing press-ups in the theatre foyer before I've finished! (*He takes out his whistle and blows three short, sharp blasts*) Hands on heads—arms folded—hands on heads—arms folded! Still! There will be total silence now for thirty seconds—nobody move!

At which point, Mullins and MacBain clatter on at the double. They have exchanged their warders' caps for police helmets. Both of them are sporting a black eye.

MacBain 'Ello, 'ello, 'ello!

Mullins 'Evening all!

MacBain What's all this 'ere?

Grummett Hang about. What do you two idiots think you're doing?

Mullins Didn't you want us on yet, Detective Constable Grummett?

Grummett I most certainly did not.

MacBain You blew your whistle.

Grummett Not for you. I only blew it because I was trying to control this gang of hooligans out there.

MacBain What scene is this then?

Grummett This is the beginning of Act Two. Buzz off, the pair of you.

Mullins and MacBain salute and turn to move off.

There's a one-eye'd yellow idol, to the north . . .

MacBain Just a minute. The beginning of Act Two?

Grummett Yes.

MacBain We are on then, right, Mr Mullins?

Mullins I thought so.

MacBain Act Two, Scene One. Most definitely. The Police Station. It's where we make our entrance. Right, Mr Mullins?

Mullins It is indeed. Act Two, Scene One. We're in the script. Enter Mullins and MacBain, a couple of comic constables, each of whom is sporting a black eye.

They both point to their black eyes.

Here's mine.

MacBain Me too. Where did you get yours from, Mr Mullins?

Mullins From the make-up lady.

MacBain So did I !

Grummett They look utterly ridiculous. What are you supposed to have black eyes for?

MacBain I had a bitter quarrel with the theatre barman in the foyer. He belted me with a Guinness bottle.

Mullins I had an altercation with an usherette at the top of the stairs—she bopped me with her torch. Ready, Mr MacBain?

MacBain Whenever you are, Mr Mullins.

Mullins You first . . .

MacBain 'Ello, 'ello, 'ello?

Mullins 'Evening all !

MacBain What's all this 'ere?

Grummett Stop acting ! Act Two, Scene One, isn't on yet. I came out here to do a prologue. There's a one-eyed yellow idol . . . (*He turns and gestures at the living-room set*) Does that *look* like police station scenery to you?

> *MacBain and Mullins turn and look at the set, then at each other, then back at Grummett.*

Well?

> *MacBain and Mullins shake their heads.*

MacBain   Not really, no.

Mullins   Not very much.

MacBain   We could tart it up to look like a cop-shop. We could paint it blue.

Mullins   Tear down the curtains.

MacBain   Put up some bars.

Mullins   Elbow the furniture.

MacBain   Rip up the carpet.

Grummett   Rip up the carpet! That is my living-room, you pair of stupid twits! You are not going to paint it blue! Neither are you ripping up the carpet! I live in it. Now buzz off back to your dressing-rooms the pair of you until the scenery changes. Go on—'op it!

> *Mullins and MacBain start to leave. Grummett calls after them.*

Just a minute!

> *Mullins and MacBain pause.*

Get those silly black eyes taken off! They make you look downright ridiculous.

> *Mullins and MacBain both put up a forefinger and touch at their eyes and then examine the ends of their fingers. The black marks corroborate that it is indeed soot. They exchange surprised glances and then make their exit. Grummett turns back to the audience.*

There's a one-eyed yellow idol, to the north of Katmandu. Now then, where had I got to? Oh yes! About cancelling the Carol Concert. Sit up straight and pay attention!

> *He blows three sharp, short blasts on his*

> *whistle to regain the audience's entire attention. Mullins and MacBain enter instantly.*

MacBain   'Ello, 'ello, 'ello!

Mullins   'Evening, all!

MacBain   What's all this 'ere?

Grummett   Not yet, not yet. I'll tell you when! Buzz off!

> *Mullins and MacBain go off. Grummet turns back to the audience.*

Grummett   During the latter half of Act One, Scene Two, a very important police officer—me—was brutally attacked. Not only that, I have discovered that these desperate criminals also nicked some personal possessions of mine, would you believe! To whit, one pair of fleecy-lined slippers and one pair of similarly fleecy-lined mittens. I intend to bring those rogues to justice. I did not catch a glimpse of the rapscallions myself—but fortunately I have a host of eye-witnesses. You lot. When I've laid my hands on all the suspects, we are going to hold an identity parade—just as soon as the stage-hands pull their fingers out, get rid of this living-room, and stick up a cop-shop on the stage. Meanwhile: There's a one-eyed yellow idol . . .

> *Clara enters.*

Clara   Stephen, Stephen Grummett! I do wish you'd give up play-acting and come down to earth!

Grummett   I'm not play-acting, dearest—I'm trying to organize a prologue.

Clara   You were trying to organize a Carol Concert five minutes ago. While you've been messing about with this panto, Stephen, we've been robbed.

Grummett   I know that, Clara. I'm trying to nick the desperadoes what have had it away with my mittens and slippers.

Clara   Never mind your mittens and slippers, Stephen. My shopping trolley's gone.

Grummett   Shopping trolley?

Clara   The one I brought into the theatre with me. With all our Christmas shopping in it.

Grummett No!

Clara Yes! The Christmas turkey *and* the Christmas crackers and the brandy for the brandy butter. Not that brandy butter would be much use to us tomorrow—we haven't got anything to put it on—the Christmas pud's been nicked as well!

Grummett What a heinous crime!

Clara I wonder if the theatre ice-cream lady has got a family-size Neapolitan tub we could have instead?

Grummett I'm not having ice-cream for my Chrissy pud!

Clara If there's no family-size Neapolitan tub it'll have to be a Cornish Double Dairy Dessert. But what's the good of getting afters if there's nothing to go before?

Grummett My Christmas dinner—hi-jacked? It's a fiendish plot. (*To the audience*) Were you little rotters in on this as well?

Clara Stop haranguing the audience, Stephen. They hadn't anything to do with it. Shouting at them won't bring our Christmas dinner back.

> *The Lights fade and the living-room set begins to move.*

Besides, it isn't safe up here—this scenery is beginning to move, I can distinctly feel it. (*She calls into the wings*) Be careful how you move this scenery. Mummy's precious darling angel boy is asleep upstairs.

> *Clara follows Grummett off. As the Lights fade up, slowly, Gilbert and Crosby return. Gilbert is still wearing the fleecy-lined slippers—he carries his own shoes stuffed in the front of his convict's blouse. Crosby is still wearing the fleecy-lined mittens.*

Gilbert Come on, Crozz. Stop moaning. Hurry up.

Crosby Are you sure there's going to be a proper Chrissy tree?

> *A Christmas tree, bigger than the one in Grummett's living-room, lights up on the police station set.*

Gilbert   Yes! Positive. Oh, look, Crozz—it's a smasher, this
           one.
Crosby   I'll bet it's still Detective Constable Grummett's
           living-room.
Gilbert   It isn't, Crozz. It's a much better tree than his. Look
           at all those lights!

           *They approach the tree. As yet, the rest of
           the police station is in darkness.*

           And look at all those sparkly things! Here—and
           there's some wrapped up prezzies underneath it,
           Crozz. I wonder who they're for.
Crosby   I'll bet it isn't me.

           *Gilbert picks up a seasonally wrapped
           parcel—which obviously contains a pair of
           handcuffs. He reads the card.*

Gilbert   'A very merry Christmas to Constable Mullins from
           his best chum, Constable MacBain.' It's a pair of
           handcuffs.

           *Crosby has also picked up a gift, seasonally
           wrapped—and not too difficult to identify.*

Crosby   'Compliments of the Season from Constable
           MacBain to his old pal, Constable Mullins. It's a
           truncheon!
Crosby }
Gilbert } *(realizing the implications)* Oooh heck!
Crosby   You've been and gone and done it again, Gilbert.
           This isn't a panto scene at all—it's the flippin'
           cop-shop. I hate police stations, Gilbert—I do, I
           really hate them.
Gilbert   Cheer up, Crozz. I promise you I'll find a proper
           tree. I will! 'Ere, Crozz—I've just had a smashing
           idea.
           Crosby covers up his ears.

           Crozzie?
Crosby   No, Gilbert. I don't want to hear it.
Gilbert   Go on, Crozzo. Just this one. I promise you you'll
           like it.
Crosby   Well—seeing as how it's Christmas. Go on—but
           make it quick, we'll have to get out of here before
           Mullins and MacBain show up.

Gilbert   They're part of my plan, Crozz. We aren't going to
          go away.
Crosby   You don't mean we're going to stay in this police
          station?
Gilbert   Yes. What are we looking for?
Crosby   Our Chrissy tree.
Gilbert   And where is it?
Crosby   We can't find it.
Gilbert   Why not?
Crosby   It's lost.
Gilbert   What do you do when you've lost something?
Crosby   You ask a copper.
Gilbert   And where do you go to *find* a copper, Crosby?
Crosby   You go to the nearest police station——
Gilbert   Well?
Crosby   Let me get this straight. You're not going to ask
          Mullins and MacBain the way to a Chrissy tree, are
          you?
Gilbert   Why not?
Crosby   Why not? Because they're policemen and we're
          desperate criminals, that's why not.
Gilbert   Do you remember when they tried to capture us
          the year before last?
Crosby   I'll say—and we got away—that was great!
Gilbert   And do you remember how we dodged them with
          those disguises on?
Crosby   Yes! That was fantastic. I had a ginger beard and
          you had a pair of specs and a big red conk.
Gilbert   What did you do with your ginger beard?
Crosby   I left it up on the shelf in the wardrobe in my
          dressing-room. What did you do with your specs
          and your big red conk?
Gilbert   I left them up on the shelf in the wardrobe in my
          dressing-room.
Crosby   Do you think they might still be there?
Gilbert   I wouldn't be at all surprised.
Crosby   Do you think they might fool Mullins and MacBain
          again?
Gilbert   I don't see why not. Come on.

> *Gilbert and Crosby exit as Detective
> Constable Grummett enters from the
> opposite side of the stage. He carries two
> rolled-up posters under his arm. He crosses
> downstage and addresses the audience.*

Grummett Right then—sit up straight and pay attention, horrors. I've managed to get things on the move at last. I have summoned reinforcements—three hundred uniformed constables from New Scotland Yard at the ratepayers' expense. They are outside in the foyer now. I can't ask them to come up on the stage as yet—they haven't got their Equity cards— but they are eager, seasoned lads, and when I give the word, they'll pounce.

> *He brandishes the rolled-up posters.*

I have also had these Identikit Wanted posters made of the villains that duffed me up and nicked my Chrissie pud, etcetera. It is my considered opinion that the evil rogues in question are not entirely dissimilar to a certain pair of missing convicts. As soon as I've nabbed 'em, I shall then get down to organizing a Constables' Carol Concert, utilizing the massed voices of the three hundred loyal lads out in the foyer—as soon as I've got 'em registered in the Variety Artists' Guild. But duty first.

> *Grummett takes out his whistle and blows
> four short, sharp blasts. There is no response.
> He tries again. Still nothing. He goes across
> and calls into the wings.*

Mullins! MacBain! Get out here smartish, on the double! (*He goes to the door*)

> *Mullins and MacBain enter slamming the
> door on Grummett. They are both wearing
> Chinese gowns and their policemen's
> helmets. Mullins is sporting a pigtail down
> his back. MacBain has a mandarin's
> flowing moustache.*

MacBain 'Erro, 'erro, 'erro!
Mullins Leveling, all!

Grummett I suppose you think that's funny. What do you pair of lunatics think you're playing at?

Mullins I'm Wishee.

MacBain I'm Washee. Out of *Aladdin*. We found these costumes in a smashing prop basket back stage.

Mullins We were only trying them on. We're supposed to be two Comical Chinese Constables from Old Kee Ping.

Grummett More like a couple of clazy clots from Clamden Clop Shop! Get out of those outfits, smartish! Not now, not now. There isn't time. Take these (*he hands them the rolled-up posters*)—and pin them up. And if anybody comes in answering those descriptions—bung them in the cells. Watch how you go—they're dangerous men. I've also seen a werewolf prowling round the theatre—it almost had me.

Mullins Do you mean a *real* werewolf, Detective Constable Grummett?

Grummett I'm of the opinion that it's a real one. But don't despair, lads. If it gives you any trouble just sing out—I've got three hundred genuine uniformed lads parading in the foyer—all eager and ready to rush to your assistance—as soon as their Equity cards turn up. *Nil desperandum.*

> *Grummett goes out, saying, 'There's a one-eyed yellow monster', etc.*

Mullins Do you know what gets me down the most? Even worse than him.

MacBain No?

Mullins Things happening on stage that didn't happen at rehearsal—like swinging this werewolf on us.

MacBain Do you remember last year's panto, Mr Mullins?

Mullins I'll never forget it. We had Count Dracula turning up out of the blue in that.

MacBain And the year before that, Frankenstein's monster arrived uninvited.

Mullins I'm applying for a transfer next Christmas, Mr MacBain.

MacBain Where to?

Mullins Toad of Toad Hall. There's nothing to put the wind

	up you in that—apart from the odd obstreporous stoat or weasel.
MacBain	Speaking for myself, next year I might have a stab at essaying the role of Mr Plod in Noddy in Toyland.

With them, we hear again the distant how of the Werewolf. The two constables dive for safety behind the counter. Gilbert and Crosby return and stand outside the police station. Gilbert is wearing a pair of joke spectacles with a false red nose attached to them. He is also wearing the fleecy-lined slippers. Crosby is wearing a joke ginger beard and the fleecy-lined mittens.

Gilbert	How do I look?
Crosby	You don't look like you at all.
Gilbert	Really?
Crosby	How about me?
Gilbert	I wouldn't recognize you, Crozz. You look like a total stranger. Go on then, in you go.
Crosby	You first
Gilbert	Come on.

They go into the police station. Mullins and MacBain emerge from behind the counter. The two convicts wearing their disguises are somewhat taken aback at the sight of Mullins and MacBain with pigtail and mandarin moustache.

Crosby	It's not a cop-shop. It's a Chinese takeaway.
MacBain	'Erro, 'erro' 'erro!
Mullins	'Leveling, all!
MacBain	What's all this 'ere?
Gilbert	Hello, hello, hello, 'evening all, what's all this 'ere! It's a cop-shop all right. Is Constable Mullins or Constable MacBain about?
MacBain	Depends who wants 'em?
Crosby	We do.
Mullins	Are you friends of theirs then?
Gilbert	(*nodding his head*) No.
Crosby	(*shaking his head*) Yes. } (*Speaking together*)

MacBain   I beg your pardon?
Gilbert   (*shaking his head*) Yes. ⎫
Crosby   (*nodding his head*) No. ⎬ (*Speaking together*)
Mullins   Would you mind repeating that?
Gilbert   He is—I'm not. ⎫
Crosby   I'm not—he is. ⎬ (*Speaking together*)
Mullins   Pardon us a minute.
MacBain   Excuse our backs.

> *MacBain and Mullins go into a huddle*
> *behind the counter. Gilbert and Crosby go*
> *into a huddle across the room. Gilbert*
> *glances across at Mullins and MacBain who*
> *are whispering together, urgently.*

Gilbert   I don't like the look of them two coppers, Crozz.
           We'll make an excuse and push off.

> *Gilbert and Crosby whisper together,*
> *urgently. MacBain glances across at them*
> *and turns to Mullins.*

MacBain   There's something fishy about those two geezers,
           Constable Mullins. We'll keep them talking until
           Detective Constable Grummett gets back.

> *The two pairs straighten up and approach*
> *each other.*

MacBain   'Ello, 'ello, 'ello!
Mullins   'Evening, all!
MacBain   Can we be of any assistance to you in your
           enquiries?
Gilbert   No thanks, if it's all the same to you.
Crosby   It's really time we were somewhere else.
Mullins   Don't rush away. We'll have a little chat with you.
MacBain   As soon as we've stuck some posters up for a
           detective friend of ours.

> *Mullins and MacBain each unroll a poster*
> *and hang them on the wall. MacBain's*
> *poster depicts a simple outline drawing of a*
> *man whose only distinguishing detail is a pair*
> *of fleecy-lined mittens. Mullins's poster*
> *shows a simple outline drawing of a man*

*whose only distinguishing feature is a pair of
fleecy-lined slippers. The two warders study
their respective posters and then turn back
to the convicts. Mullins looks at Gilbert
while MacBain looks at Crosby.*

Mullins   (*to Gilbert*) Now then, what was it you wanted?
MacBain   (*to Crosby*) Is there anything we can do to help?

*At which point, Mullins realizes that
Gilbert is wearing slippers while MacBain
becomes aware that Crosby is wearing
mittens.*

Mullins   (*to Gilbert*) Just a moment.
MacBain   (*to Crosby*) Hang about.

*The warders turn and look at their
respective posters again. They glance back
at the convicts and then back at their
posters. While Mullins and Macbain stare at
their separate posters a second time,
Gilbert takes off his slippers and gives them
to Crosby; Crosby hands Gilbert his mittens.
Gilbert puts on the mittens; Crosby puts on
the slippers. Mullins turns back to Gilbert;
MacBain turns back to Crosby.*

Mullins   That's funny!
MacBain   How very odd!
Mullins   (*to Gilbert*) Weren't you wearing a pair of
             fleecy-lined slippers?
Gilbert   Not me.
MacBain   (*to Crosby*) Didn't you have on a pair of
             fleecy-lined mittens?
Crosby   Not to my knowledge.
MacBain   Just a moment.
Mullins   Hang about.

*The warders turn back to look at their
posters again, but this time they change
positions. Mullins looks at the 'mittens'
poster while MacBain turns to the 'slippers'
one. Mullins turns back to Crosby. MacBain
turns back to Gilbert.*

MacBain   Very strange.
Mullins   Most peculiar.
MacBain   Don't go away.
Mullins   Hang on.

> *Again the warders refer to the posters:
> Mullins 'mittens'; MacBain 'slippers'. Again
> Gilbert and Crosby exchange mittens and
> slippers and put them on. They also change
> places. When the warders turn, MacBain
> confronts Crosby who is wearing the
> mittens, while Mullins is facing Gilbert who
> is wearing the slippers.*

MacBain   I don't get this at all.
Mullins   There's something extremely fishy going on. (*To
          Gilbert*) Do you mind if I have a look at those
          slippers?
MacBain   Can I examine those mittens?

> *Gilbert hands Mullins the slippers. Crosby
> hands MacBain the mittens. Again the
> warders consult their posters: MacBain
> 'slippers', Mullins 'mittens'. They then turn
> and study each other. MacBain sees only a
> man holding a pair of slippers; Mullins is
> only aware of a man holding a pair of
> mittens.*

MacBain   You're in possession of a pair of wanted
          fleecy-lined slippers!
Mullins   You're holding on to a pair of stolen fleecy-lined
          mittens!

> *MacBain and Mullins grapple with each
> other, trying to effect an arrest. Gilbert
> snatches at their opportunity.*

Gilbert   Come on, Crozz—now's our chance—run for it!

> *Gilbert and Crosby flee into the audience.
> MacBain and Mullins realize their mistake,
> but it is too late— they are handcuffed to
> each other. They manage to take out their
> whistles and blow several short, sharp
> blasts. Grummett enters and spots Gilbert*

*and Crosby making for the rear of the
auditorium. He bellows at the audience.*

Grummett Stop them ! Seize those men !

*But Gilbert and Crosby escape into the
foyer. Grummett turns back to Mullins and
MacBain.*

You pair of fat-headed blitherin' nincompoops !
You've done it again ! You've let two desperate
criminals escape !

Mullins   We were only doing our best.

MacBain   We got carried away, Detective Constable
Grummett, with enthusiasm.

Mullins   We always do.

MacBain   We're at our best as a panto horse.

Mullins gets into his panto-horse position.

Not now.

Grummett Shut up ! Get off the stage ! Get those handcuffs
off. Go on.

Mullins   I haven't got my key but he has.

MacBain   I left mine at home in my other trousers.

Grummett Get someone in Stage Management to give you a
hand.

MacBain and Mullins exit sheepishly.

Grummett (*addressing the audience*) And you lot ought to be
ashamed of yourselves as well. Talk about asking
the general public to 'have a go'. You deliberately
allowed those desperate criminals to run right past
you. Well, I'll tell you this much—you're going to
suffer now. There's a one-eyed yellow monster to
the north of Katmandu, etc.

*He is interrupted by Brenda Prendergast, the
ice-cream girl, making her way towards the
stage from the rear of the auditorium.
Brenda wears a white overall, white
plimsolls, and carries her ice-cream tray.*

Brenda   Excuse me ! I say ! Can I have a word ?

Grummett Are you addressing me, Madam ?

Brenda   Are you Detective Constable Grummett from New
Scotland Yard ?

Grummett What if I am? What do you want? Who are you?
Brenda I've got a message for you. I'm the ice-cream girl.
Grummett Come down here. Come on!

Brenda approaches the stage.

I can see you're the ice-cream girl. I mean, what's your name?
Brenda It's Brenda.
Grummett Isn't there any more of it? Brenda what?
Brenda Brenda Prendergast. That's Gast, G-A-S-T not G-A-S-S-E-D.

Grummett has taken out his notebook and makes an entry in it.

Grummett It's all right. I can spell.
Brenda 'Ere, what are you writing my name down for?
Grummett Never you mind, my girl. Official business. What about this message. (*Indicating the stage*) Come up here.
Brenda I can't.
Grummett Why not?
Brenda I'm not allowed up there. I'm only the ice-cream girl. I'm not in the panto.
Grummett I'm not in it either, missis. Do I *look* like a flippin' actor? Don't give me a hard time, young lady. Do as you're told—jump up.
Brenda I've already said—I can't.
Grummett 'Ere? Have you got something to hide?
Brenda 'Course I haven't—but if I get up on that stage them lights will make my ice-creams go all soft and soggy. I'll lose my job.
Grummett If you don't get up here, smartish, young woman, I shall lose my temper—and then there will be trouble. For the last time, up here, or I shall nick you on suspicion. Move!

Brenda joins Grummett on the stage.

That's a bit more like it. What's all this mullarkey about a message?
Brenda Do you know them three hundred coppers that are out there in the foyer?

Grummett   Not individually, no. But I know *of* them. They're
           parading under my explicit instructions.
Brenda   No, they're not. They're not parading at all. They're
           lounging about and noshing ice-creams. 'Ere, they
           can't half put them back! A hundred and fifty-two
           raspberry ripple tubs; seventy-eight orange flavour
           Spiderman Icicle-pops; and three dozen midnight
           mint choc-lollies. I've emptied my tray three times.
Grummett   Never mind your sales figures, young woman. What
           about this message?
Brenda   Oh, yes! Do you know, it's completely slipped my
           mind.
Grummett   Come along, young woman. Think! Think!
Brenda   I'm trying. I can remember the policeman who gave
           it to me. I can see him as clear as day—a big tall
           sergeant with some raspberry ripple on his chin and
           an orange-flavour icicle-pop stain down the front
           of his tunic——
Grummett   What was the message!
Brenda   Don't shout—you'll only confuse me.
Grummett   What about the message?
Brenda   I've got it. He said to tell you that the three
           hundred policemen had apprehended two suspicious
           characters who ran out of the auditorium into the
           foyer.
Grummett   Did he happen to mention their descriptions?
Brenda   One of them has a ginger beard and the other one's
           got a big red conk and a pair of funny spectacles.
Grummett   Them's 'em! We've got 'em! Where are they now?
Brenda   He said to tell you he's had two of his men take them
           round and leave them for you at the stage door.
Grummett   That's it. Case closed. I'll get Mullins and MacBain
           to bring 'em on. (*Indicating the audience*) And
           then this lot out here can identify 'em. Mullins!
           MacBain!

                    *He takes out his whistle and blows several
                    short, sharp blasts. A panto horse gallops
                    on to the stage and into the police station.*

Grummett   Mullins! MacBain! I know you're in there. Get out
           of that panto horse and back in uniform at once. I
           want those prisoners brought on.

The horse executes several circuits of the stage and finally nuzzles up to Brenda.

Brenda   Aw! He's after my Raspberry Ripples. Is it all right if I give him one?

Grummett No! I want the prisoners brought on.

The horse whispers in Brenda's ear.

What does it say?

Brenda   It says it'll bring the prisoners on after you've asked it to do a sum.

Grummett I asked it a sum last year and it got it wrong. (*To the horse*) Get off!

The horse whispers again in Brenda's ear.

Brenda   It says its taken its 'Hay Levels' this year. Ask it what three times three is?

Grummett No!

The horse crosses its front hooves, implacably, and tosses its head. Grummett is forced to concede.

Grummett Oh, very well. What's three times three?

The horse stamps its hoof on the ground ten times.

That was ten. It's got it wrong again! Get off this stage!

MacBain   No it wasn't.

Mullins   Yes it was.

The horse goes off, hanging its head in shame.

Brenda   Can I get off as well?

Grummett No, you can't. I need your help up here.

Brenda   What about my ices? They're turning into a gooey pool of sticky stuff. I've got to go—I'll get the bullet.

Grummett You're going nowhere, young woman, until I've identified two desperate criminals. I'm holding you for further questioning. (*He nods into the wings*) You can wait up there until I'm ready for you.

Brenda   Oooh!

> *Brenda goes off as Grummett crosses
> downstage and addresses the audience.*

Grummett   This is the bit I've been waiting for. The
Identification Parade. This is where you bunch of
idle herberts start to earn your keep. You're going to
help me identify the desperate criminals, aren't you,
kids?

Audience   No!

Grummett   Yes, you are! Don't cheek me, you little horrors.
This is what you're here for. Mullins! MacBain!
March in the line of suspects.

> *Behind Grummet's back, Mullins and
> MacBain escort Gilbert and Crosby into the
> police station. Gilbert is still wearing his
> false nose and glasses; Crosby has on the
> ginger beard. Grummett continues to the
> audience without looking round.*

Sit up straight, pay attention—this is serious. I want
you to study, carefully, this line of men behind me
and shout out if you see anyone you recognize.
Take your time—examine all their faces——

> *He breaks off, reacting to a yell from the
> audience.*

There's what? Only two of who? (*He turns and
studies the line-up*) Mullins! MacBain! What's
going on? Where's all the other suspects?

Mullins   This is it, Detective Constable Grummett.

Grummett   Two? Two! Flippin' two! I can't have an
identification line-up with just two suspects. (*To
Gilbert*) Have you always worn funny specs and
had a big red conk?

Gilbert   Ever since I can remember.

Grummett   And have you always had a ginger beard?

Crosby   I was born with one.

Grummett   (*to Mullins and MacBain*) Don't stand there
dithering. Go and send a few more actors on—as
many as you can find with ginger beards and big red
conks.

MacBain   There aren't any more, Detective Constable
Grummett.

Mullins   These are all there is.

Grummett That is ridiculous! What a cheapjack production!
I can't carry on up here without a few suspicious
faces in my line-up. Mullins, nip out into the
audience and see what you can rustle up. They
don't come any more suspicious-looking than that
lot out there. Look at 'em—like the cast of a horror
film.

MacBain I can't see many out there with big red conks and
ginger beards, Detective Constable Grummett.

Grummett Use your imagination, MacBain. This is a police
station, isn't it? There must be a box of detective
disguises somewhere—dish some ginger beards and
big red conks up out of that. Jump to it, MacBain!

> *MacBain produces a large box labelled
> 'DETECTIVES' DISGUISES' from behind the
> counter. The box contains a selection of
> cheap false moustaches; joke red noses;
> beards, etc. Mullins goes into the audience
> and selects a half-dozen children. He
> escorts the children on to the stage where
> MacBain hands them each a 'disguise'.
> Grummett organizes his identity parade of
> eight suspects, including Gilbert and
> Crosby, each, of whom is now wearing
> some sort of disguise. At last, Grummett
> steps back and admires the end result.*

Grummett Gordon Bennett—I've seen some Rogues' Galleries
lined up before, but this lot takes the chocolate
biscuit—I've never known an Identity Parade as
evil and 'orrible as this one before.

MacBain A 'ighly suspicious-looking bunch of characters.
What's your opinion, Mr Mullins?

Mullins I wouldn't trust one single one of 'em as far as I
could throw him, Mr MacBain. (*Pointing at the
smallest suspect*) Especially that one there. He
looks partickerlerly 'orrible.

Grummett Stand up straight. No slouching. Hands out of
pockets, eyes front, nobody move unless I give the
word. Still!

> *Grummett moves down to face the audience.
> Gilbert and Crosby are on the right-hand
> side of the line of children.*

Grummett Pay attention, you lot. I don't want any messing about. This is a very serious business. Because, depending upon the evidence that you are about to give, a couple of these villains standing here behind me will be having their Christmas scoff in clink. (*He addresses the audience*) Now, can any of you keen-eyed kids spot the real villains in this line-up? Come on—hands up anybody who can tell me which of them are the genuine one-hundred-percent desperate criminals?

> *Grummett, taking his cues from the instructions of the audience, goes into a routine of false identifications. When the audience assure him that Gilbert and Crosby are on the right-hand end of the line (and therefore his left), Grummett stretches out his left hand, and says, 'This end?' as he faces the audience. Receiving their confirmation, he turns, keeping his left hand extended, and promptly places his hands on the shoulders of the two children on the left-hand end of the line-up.*

Grummett These ones?
Audience No! No! The other end—etc.

> *And as Grummett turns to face the audience, Gilbert and Crosby switch positions to the left-hand end of the line-up, and the above procedure is repeated, with Grummett making another wrongful arrest. Eventually, and again while Grummett's back is turned, Gilbert and Crosby, shuffling children around like wild-fire, take up a position in the centre of the line-up. Grummett, again taking his instructions from the audience, turns to arrest them. But the two convicts have again shuffled themselves and their fellow suspects around and are standing somewhere else. Grummett takes a firm hold on the collars of the two children in the centre of the row.*

Grummett It's these ones, is it? Yes, you don't surprise me—
I've had my eye on these rapscallions from the very

moment they stepped up. Mr Mullins, Mr MacBain
—take hold of them and put them in the pokey.
Careful now, they're desperate criminals both of
'em.

> *Grummett hands the two children over to*
> *Mullins and MacBain who make as if to*
> *lead them away. Then, while the attention*
> *of the detective and his two constables is*
> *directed elsewhere, and during the*
> *protestations against wrongful arrest from*
> *the audience, Gilbert and Crosby snatch at*
> *their opportunity—*

Gilbert   Now's our chance, Crozz—run for it!

> *—and the two convicts discard their*
> *disguises and take to their heels. Grummett*
> *spots them.*

Grummett Stop! Stop! That's them! Gilbert and Crosby!
They've got away. You're holding on to two
entirely innocent members of the audience.
Release them.

> *During the following speech, Mullins and*
> *MacBain usher the line-up 'suspects' back*
> *to their seats, allowing them to keep their*
> *'disguises'.*

Grummett (*to the audience*) I blame you lot. You were telling
fibs. Providing an officer of New Scotland Yard
with false information—that's perjury is that. You
could get fiteen years apiece—you will get fifteen
years apiece——

> *The Lights begin to fade.*

Hang about. What's happening to the lights?
Mullins, MacBain!

> *Grummett disappears into the back of the*
> *stage. Mullins and MacBain come back on*
> *to the stage from the auditorium.*

MacBain Come on, we're doing a bunk, the scenery's
changing.

Mullins   We're getting off before the spooky bit!

> *Mullins and MacBain exit. The police*

> *station is transformed (in full view of the
> audience) into a spooky wood. Gilbert and
> Crosby return.*

Crosby   This way, Gillo—come *on*! I don't like the look of
         this scenery, Gilbert. Not one little bit.
Gilbert Stop moaning, Crozzo.
Crosby   We escaped from the clutches of the law—what
         are we coming back on for now?
Gilbert To do what we set out to do—to look for the
         Chrissy tree, Crozz. Our tree.
Crosby   What makes you think we're going to find it here?
Gilbert It's got to be here—you always find what you're
         looking for before the final curtain falls. It must be
         here.
Crosby   There's plenty of trees all right—but it doesn't look
         much like panto scenery. It's a bit too spooky.

> *At which point, with them, we hear again
> the howl of the Werewolf away in the
> distance. A host of scarey eyes light up and
> peer at them from the depths of the wood.*

         You stupid, raving idiot, Gilly! You've led us to a
         tree all right. A woodful of trees—it's the Werewolf's
         wood you've got us into this time.
Gilbert It isn't, Crozz. It can't be.
Crosby   It's the Werewolf's wood, Gilbert. And any moment
         now it'll spring out and get us.
Gilbert Shut up, Crozz. I don't think it is the Werewolf's
         wood. You don't have werewolves' woods in pantos.
Crosby   You don't have spooky staring eyes in pantos—but
         we've got a forest full of them here.

> *There is a Lighting change and the scary
> eyes disappear.*

Gilbert Don't be afraid of them, Crozzo—they're going
         anyway. Hey, Crozz! I've suddenly tumbled to
         where we are. It isn't a werewolf's wood at all—it's
         Cinderella's forest scenery.
Crosby   Cinderella's forest?
Gilbert Yeh! You remember. Where Cinderella's out
         collecting firewood for the Ugly Sisters, and she

meets this old woman picking up dry tinder from the forest floor.

Crosby   Are you sure?

Gilbert   Positive. Look—what did I tell you—here comes the fairy godmother now.

A bent figure, hooded in a dark cloak, enters picking up sticks from the ground.

Crosby   You're right, Gillo! We're saved. Ask her if she knows the way out of this scenery back to the dressing-rooms.

Gilbert approaches the bent figure.

Gilbert   Excuse me, old woman. My name is Gilbert and this is Crosby. I wonder if you could help us? We're trying to find our way out of this scenery back to the dressing-rooms.

Figure   I'm ever so sorry, no. I'm a stranger here myself.

Crosby   Aren't you Cinderella's fairy godmother?

The figure throws off her cloak, revealing herself as Brenda Prendergast, the ice-cream girl.

Brenda   I wish I was. I'm the ice-cream lady from the foyer.

Gilbert   What are you doing up here then? Picking up dry tinder from the forest floor?

Brenda   I wasn't. I was picking up ice-lolly sticks. I put this cloak on so's I wouldn't be noticed.

She bursts into tears.

Gilbert   What's the matter?

Brenda   I'll get the bullet now for sure!

Gilbert   No, you won't. What for?

Brenda   I was only trying to do my job proper—until that detective fetched me up on the stage and made me stand over there. Then the lights turned all my ices into a sticky puddle. And then the scenery started to move and jogged my arm and my ice-lolly sticks went flying all over the forest floor.

Gilbert   Don't cry, gel. If they give you the sack out there, you can come up here for good and be in the panto with Croz and me.

Brenda's tears vanish immediately.

Brenda   Can I really? Do you promise?

Gilbert   'Course you can. Can't she, Crozz?

Crosby   I dunno. I'm not so sure.

Brenda   Go on. Let me. That's what I came to London for.
          To be an actress. I used to be a petrol-pump
          attendant on the Guildford by-pass.

Gilbert   Why did you give it up?

Brenda   I had a row with my boyfriend, Reg. He's a chef, is
          Reg, in a Wimpy Bar just off the M-four. I wanted
          to prove to him I could get my name in lights.
          Brenda Prendergast—that's G-A-S-T, not
          G-A-S-S-E-D—in *Jack and the Beanstalk*. Brenda
          Prendergast in *Aladdin and His Wonderful Lamp*. I
          can do it, too. I've got the costume. I found it out
          there.

          *She takes off her ice-cream girl's overall to
          reveal that underneath she is wearing a
          pantomime fairy-queen's costume.*

Brenda   Watch this. *Jack and the Beanstalk——*

          She strikes a pose.

Dear kindly Jack,
Your Magic Beans,
Shall touch the sky,
I have the means——

          *She breaks off and comes out of character
          as she realizes that her costume is
          incomplete.*

Hold your horses. I'm sure there was a wand to go
with this outfit.

          *She locates her wand, possibly from behind
          a tree. She fiddles with it for a moment.*

I think it's supposed to light up—but it must need
a battery. I'll try again. *Jack and the Beanstalk——*

          Again, she strikes her pose.

Dear kindly Jack,
Your Magic Beans,
Shall touch the sky,

I have the means,
My fairy wand,
Will make them grow,
One gentle wave,
And off they go!

Aladdin and his Wonderful Lamp——
(*more forcefully*)

Fear not, Aladdin,
Tho' thou art,
Left in this cave,
And in the cart,
Old Abanazar's end,
Is now in sight,
My magic fairy wand,
Will put *his* evil deeds to flight!

> *And then to Gilbert and Crosby——*

How was it? Do I get the part?

Gilbert   Not bad. I've seen worse.

Crosby   I haven't. It was awful.

Brenda   Go on, let me be in it. I'll be ever so good. I can see my name in lights now—Brenda Prendergast in——

> *At which point we hear again the howl of the Werewolf.*

Brenda   'Brenda Prendergast meets the Werewolf!'

> *The Lights fade and again we see the scary eyes in the forest.*

It's not a *real* werewolf, is it?

Gilbert   We think it might be. Can't you get that wand of yours to work and magic it away?

> *Brenda fiddles with her wand.*

Brenda   Not without a battery. There's hardly any magic left in it at all.

Gilbert   A tiny bit of magic might be enough, if we had something else as well. Something that would scare it.

Crosby   You can't scare a werewolf, Gilly.

Gilbert   We scared away Dracula last year.

Crosby	Hey, you're right, Gilly. We did! With a grinning green skelligog. And we scared away Frankenstein's monster the year before.
Gilbert	With a horrible hairy spider.

The howl of the Werewolf is heard again, louder than before.

Brenda	It's getting closer!
Crosby	Oh, Gilly! If only we had the skelligog and the spider this year!
Gilbert	I'll bet they're up there somewhere. Crosby. If only we knew how to bring them on.

The audience is shouting out instructions.

Do you remember, kids? We did what? We shouted 'Wheee!' for the grinning green skelligog and 'Whooo!' for the horrible hairy spider. Have you got that, Crozz? That's right. Will you shout them out and help us give the Werewolf the jim-jams, kids?

Audience: 'Yes!'

Smashin'! This is what we'll do then. When the Werewolf comes on, I'll drop my hand like this— that's the signal for you to shout out 'Wheee!' That'll bring the skelly on.

Crosby	Then when I drop my hand again, you shout 'Whooo!' That'll bring the spider on.
Gilbert	Then, when the Werewolf's staggering about, with a severe attack of the screaming jim-jams, Brenda can wave her wand at it and you all shout out 'Vanish, Werewolf!'
Crosby	Do you think that'll do it, Gilly?
Gilbert	It's worth a try. Shall we have a practice, kids? Crosby, you pretend to be the Werewolf. Remember, kids, one hand, 'Wheee!', second hand, 'Whooo!' and when Brenda waves her wand—'Vanish, Werewolf!'

Gilbert and Brenda hide. Crosby staggers on, pretending to be the Werewolf. They go through the routine.

That was great, kids! I'm sure that'll——

The howl of the Werewolf yet again,
louder than ever.

Crosby   He's here, Gilly.
Gilbert   Quick! Hide!

The trio hide. The Werewolf enters. Gilbert
drops his hand. The Audience shout
'Whee!' The skeleton drops in. The
Werewolf staggers back. Gilbert drops his
other hand. The Audience shout
'Whoo!' The spider drops in. The
Werewolf staggers back again. Brenda
enters and waves her wand at the
Werewolf. The Audience shout 'Vanish,
Werewolf!' The Werewolf reacts with
surprise, and removes its werewolf mask.

Werewolf   Brenda!
Brenda   Reggie!
Crosby   Who?
Brenda   Reggie!
Gilbert
Crosby   }Who's Reggie?
Brenda   It's my boyfriend, Reggie. Fancy seeing you here.
            Dressed up as a werewolf.
Reggie   I came to Camden to look for you, Brenda. I
            thought you'd have your name in lights by now.
Brenda   (*shaking her head*) I'm only the ice-cream lady in
            the foyer, Reggie. I couldn't get a job as an actress.
            I thought you were grilling hamburgers in a Wimpy
            Bar off the M-four?
Reggie   I gave it up. I got a job as an actor, Brenda, to look
            for you.
Gilbert   You're not a *real* actor, are you?
Reggie   Yes, I am. I'm a famous one.
Crosby   You haven't even got your name in the programme.
Reggie   Yes, I have.
Gilbert
Crosby   }No, you haven't.
Reggie   Yes, I have. Not as the Werewolf, no. I've got two
            parts. (*He produces a moustache from his pocket*)
            I'm down in the programme as the Prison Governor.
Brenda   (*impressed*) Was that you as well, Reg? Crikey!

Reggie   (*modestly*) I play *three* parts actually, Bren. I also appear as Reggie, a Wimpy Bar chef just off the M-four.

Brenda   Flippin' heckers! You aren't half clever, Reggie!

Reggie   I thought you were good as the Fairy Queen.

Brenda   I'm not in your class though. I could never play three parts in one production. I'm giving this side of the footlights up, Reggie. One person with his name in lights is more than enough for one family.

They embrace.

Gilbert   I liked her, Crozz.

Crosby   I must admit I've seen worse.

Gilbert   I wouldn't have minded winning her hand, myself.

Crosby   You? No chance, Gillo. You're a desperate criminal. Desperate criminals never finish up winning the hands of beautiful ice-cream ladies from the auditorium.

Gilbert   No. Still—we've finished up free. It's very nearly a happy ending.

Detective Constable Grummett enters.

Grummett No, it isn't. Nowhere near. Arrests are pending.

He takes out his whistle and blows several short, sharp blasts. MacBain and Mullins enter, dressed as the Ugly Sisters, but wearing their police helmets and carrying their truncheons.

MacBain   'Ello, 'ello, 'ello!

Mullins   'Evening all!

MacBain   What's all this 'ere?

Grummett Who the naff do you think you've come as now?

MacBain   The Ugly Sisters.

Mullins   Isn't this Cinderella's Wood, Detective Constable Grummett?

Grummett No it isn't. It's going to be a Carol Concert. I've got three hundred uniformed lads outside the stage door.

MacBain }
Mullins } We hope there's two for us.

Grummett No, there isn't. As soon as I've tied up the loose ends and solved the mystery of the missing Christmas turkey . . .

MacBain We've done that for you, Detective Constable Grummett?

Grummett You've what?

Mullins We know who nicked Missis Grummett's shopping-trolley.

> *MacBain goes over to the wings and leads on Alexander Grummett by his ear. Alexander is carrying—or balanced on—a skateboard.*

Grummett You know who nicked Missis Grummet's shopping-trolley.

MacBain Come on, you little villain—let's be having you.

Grummett Alexander? My lad? My flesh and blood? A copper's son? Nicked his own mother's shopping-trolley?

Alexander Only the wheels, Dad. I wanted them for my skateboard. Only 'cos you said I couldn't have one. I can still have the Martian deathray pistol, can't I, Dad? And the razor-sharp Samurai sword and the South American headhunter's blow-pipe with the poisoned arrows?

Grummett Where's my turkey? What have you done with that? You little devil, you'll get a clip round the lug-hole——

> *Clara Grummett enters, carrying a tray piled high with hamburgers.*

Clara You lay one finger on that boy, Stephen Grummett, and you'll have me to answer to. Here's your Christmas turkey.

Grummett Where?

Clara There!

Grummett There?

Clara These. (*Indicating Reggie*) I was talking to this nice kind gentleman in the interval. He showed me how to make it into turkey burgers.

Grummett My Christmas turkey! My Christmas dinner! A

turkey burger! (*To Reggie*) You'll get fifteen years
for this.

Clara   Oh, do stop moaning, Stephen. It's Christmas. Try
           one.
                   *Grummett takes a turkeyburger and nibbles
                   at it.*

Grummett Hey! They're not bad, are they?
Clara   There you are you see. Come on, Alexy-walexy,
           let's get back to our real replica living-room, and
           let the proper actors finish off the play.

                   Clara and Alexander exit.

Grummett Come on, Mullins and MacBain.
Mullins   Where are we going to, Detective Constable
           Grummett?
Grummett St Pancras Station. For the Carol Concert. I can't
           disappoint three hundred coppers.
Mullins ⎫
MacBain ⎭ And neither can we!
                   Mullins and MacBain exit singing.

Grummett (*to Reggie*) You want to give this acting lark up,
           mate. Get a job making turkeyburgers. They're
           advertising for a chef in a Wimpy Bar just off the
           M-four.

Brenda   We're going one better than that. We're going into
           partnership. We're going to open Swindon's first
           and foremost combined turkeyberger bar and ice-
           cream parlour. Tarra!

Reggie   Tarra!
                   Reggie and Brenda exit.

Grummett Hey, this isn't a real turkeyburger. It's a replica of
           one.
                   He exits

Gilbert   That's it then, Crozz, for another year.
Crosby   Yes. You managed to do it again, Gilbert.
Gilbert   What's that?
Crosby   Let me down. We didn't find the Chrissy tree you
           promised.
Gilbert   Never mind, Crozzy. We've got our freedom. They

can't put us back in clink. The Prison Governor's packed it in to make turkeyburgers.

Gilbert has picked up the fairy wand that Brenda has left behind.

Crosby   You don't suppose it does work, do you?

Gilbert   No. It isn't a real one, Crozz. It's only a prop. Besides, you heard what she said. It needs a battery.

Crosby   Supposing we blew on it?

Gilbert   Blew on it? Don't be daft. What for? It's a piece of wood.

Crosby   Supposing—supposing everybody blew on it?

Gilbert   The audience?

Crosby nods

Do you want to try it, kids? Just to please Crosby?

Audience   Yes!

Gilbert   When I say three then. One, two, three!

The audience blows

I think I saw a spark.

Crosby   So did I, Gilly! I think it's going to work. Blow harder, kids!

Gilbert   Come on, kids, altogether—when I say three— One. Two. Three!

The audience blows again. The wand lights up.

Crosby   We've done it, Gilbert! Wave it now! Perform some magic!

Gilbert waves the fairy wand. The central tree in the forest begins to glow and is transformed into a Christmas tree.

Fantastic, Gilly!

Gilbert   Terrific, Crozzo!

Gilbert   It's our Christmas tree, Crozzie.

Crosby   What Gilbert? The one we've been looking for?

Gilbert   We've found it, Crozz! *Our* Tree! A Merry
           Christmas, Crozz!
Crosby   A Merry Christmas, Gillo!
Together   A Merry Christmas, kids, and a Happy New Year!

CURTAIN

www.ingramcontent.com/pod-product-compliance
Ingram Content Group UK Ltd.
Pitfield, Milton Keynes, MK11 3LW, UK
UKHW021822150726
7214IPUK00017B/274